CATS

MAINE COON CATS

STUART A. KALLEN
ABDO & Daughters

Published by Abdo & Daughters, 4940 Viking Drive, Suite 622, Edina, Minnesota 55435.

Library bound edition distributed by Rockbottom Books, Pentagon Tower, P.O. Box 36036, Minneapolis, Minnesota 55435.

Cover Photo credit: Peter Arnold, Inc.
Interior Photo credits: Peter Arnold, Inc. pages 9, 11, 13

Animals, Animals, pages 15, 17, 19, 21

Edited by Rosemary Wallner

Library of Congress Cataloging-in-Publication Data

Kallen, Sutart A., 1955
    Maine coon cat / Stuart A. Kallen.
     p. cm. — (Cats)
Includes bibliographical references (p. 24) and index.
    Summary: Presents information about the oldest and largest
American breed of cat including physical characteristics, care and feeding, and what
to look for when buying a kitten.
    ISBN 1-56239-448-7
l. Maine coon cat—Juvenile literature. [1. Maine coon cat. 2. Cats.] I. Title. II. Series:
Kallen, Stuart A., 1955- Cats.
SF449.M34K35   1995
636.8'3—dc20
           95-12656
           CIP
           AC

ABOUT THE AUTHOR
Stuart Kallen has written over 80 children's books, including many environmental science books.

Contents

LIONS, TIGERS, AND CATS

Few animals are as beautiful and graceful as cats. And all cats are related. From the wild lions of Africa to the common house cat, all belong to the family **Felidae**. Cats are found almost everywhere. They include cheetahs, jaguars, lynx, ocelots, and **domestic** cats.

THE MIDDLE EAST

Turkey

Lebanon
Syria
Israel
Iraq
Iran (Persia)

Egypt
Jordan
United Arab Emirates

Kuwait

Qatar

Saudi Arabia

Oman

Yemen

People first **domesticated** cats around 5,000 years ago in the Middle East. Although humans have **tamed** them, house cats still think and act like their bigger cousins.

All cats—from cheetahs to the domestic house cat—are related.

THE MAINE COON CAT

The Maine coon cat is the oldest and largest American **breed**. It is the second most popular cat breed in the United States.

Many people believe that these animals were once wild cats living in the state of Maine. Their early **ancestors** were probably farm cats and longhaired cats that traders and sailors brought to Maine. The first Maine coon cat was registered at a show in New York City in 1861.

The early ancestors of the Maine coon cat were probably brought to Maine by traders and sailors.

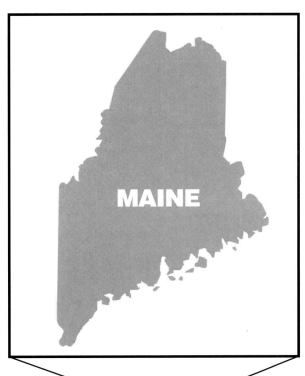

MAINE

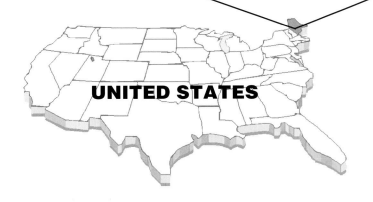

UNITED STATES

Detail Area

WHAT THEY'RE LIKE

Sailors probably brought Maine coon cats to sea to control mice on ships. These cats have a strange habit of "sleeping rough," which means they can be found curled up in funny positions in small nooks. Maine coons make a quiet chirping sound and are sweet, loving pets.

The Maine coon is an affectionate cat.

COAT AND COLOR

Many Maine coon cats have markings like those on raccoons. The cats developed thick coats to protect them from the harsh New England winters. Their fur is long and silky, and they have flowing tail fur.

Maine coon cats come in many colors including white, black, blue and white, silver tabby, and brown tabby. In all, there are thirty different kinds of Maine coon cats. People have recorded over sixty color combinations.

Many Maine coon cats have thick coats and markings like those on raccoons.

SIZE

Maine coon cats are large, long, and well-muscled. Some males weigh as much as eighteen pounds (8 kg). Their paws are large and round, and they have a broad chest.

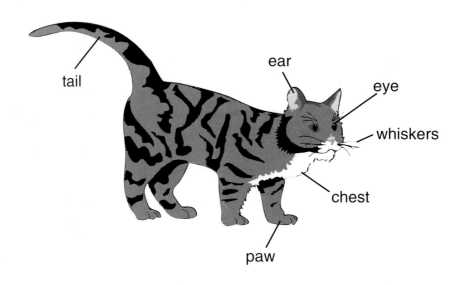

Most cats share the same features.

Maine coon cats are large, long, and muscular.

CARE

Maine coons are strong and independent. But with their long hair, they need a good brushing at least once a week. Besides making the cat purr, brushing a Maine coon will keep its loose hair off the furniture. **Grooming** a Maine coon will also keep **hair balls** from forming.

Like any pet, Maine coon cats need a lot of love and attention. Cats make fine pets. But Maine coons still have some of their wild **instincts**.

Cats are natural hunters and do well exploring outdoors. A scratching post where the cat can sharpen its claws saves furniture from damage.

Cats bury their waste and should be trained to use a litter box. Clean the box every day.

Cats love to play. A ball, **catnip**, or a loose string will keep a kitten busy for hours.

A Maine coon cat grooming itself.

FEEDING

Cats eat meat and fish. Hard bones that do not splinter help keep their teeth and mouth clean. Water should always be available. Most cats enjoy dried cat food. Kittens enjoy their mother's milk. However, milk can cause illness in full-grown cats.

Cats are meat eaters. This cat is eating dried cat food.

KITTENS

Female cats are **pregnant** for about sixty-five days. They will have two to eight kittens. The average cat has four kittens.

Kittens are blind and helpless for the first several weeks. After about three weeks, they will start crawling and playing. At this time they may be given cat food.

After about a month, kittens will run, wrestle, and play games. If the cat is a **pedigree**, it should be registered and given papers at this time. At ten weeks, the kittens are old enough to be sold or given away.

A Maine coon kitten.

BUYING A KITTEN

The best place to get a Maine coon cat is from a **breeder**. Cat shows are also good places to find kittens.

Next, you must decide if you want a pet or a show winner. A Maine coon cat can cost about $50, with blue-ribbon winners costing as much as $500. When you buy a Maine coon, you should get **pedigree** papers that register the animal with the Cat Fanciers Association.

When buying a kitten, check it closely for signs of good health. The ears, nose, mouth, and fur should be clean. Eyes should be bright and clear. The cat should be alert and interested in its surroundings. A healthy kitten will move around with its head held high.

A Maine coon cat.

GLOSSARY

ANCESTOR - An animal from which other animals are directly descended.

BREEDER - A person who breeds animals or plants.

CATNIP - A strong-smelling plant used as stuffing for cat toys.

DOMESTICATE (doe-MESS-tih-kate) - To tame or adapt to home life.

FELIDAE (FEE-lih-day) - The Latin name given to the cat family.

GROOMING - Cleaning.

HAIR BALLS - Balls of fur that gather in a cat's stomach after grooming itself by licking.

INSTINCT - A way of acting that is born in an animal, not learned.

NON-PEDIGREE (non-PED-ih-gree) - An animal without a record of its ancestors.

PEDIGREE (PED-ih-gree) - A record of an animal's ancestors.

PREGNANT - With one or more babies growing inside the body.

TAME - To reduce from a wild to a domestic state.

Index

BIBLIOGRAPHY

Alderton, David. *Cats*. New York: Dorling Kindersley, 1992.

Clutton-Brock, Juliet. *Cat*. New York: Alfred A. Knopf, 1991.

DePrisco, Andrew. *The Mini-Atlas of Cats*. Neptune City, N.J.: T.F.H. Publications, 1991.

Taylor, David. *The Ultimate Cat Book*. New York: Simon & Schuster, 1989.